Tracing Your IRISH Ancestors

Peggy Magee

Copyright ©1986 by Peggy Magee

Published by

Magee Publications
P. O. Box 26507
Prescott Valley, AZ 86312

First Printing, April, 1986

ISBN 0-937267-13-9

Printed in U.S.A.

Table of Contents

Forward

Twenty-five years ago as a young man I entered an archives intending to do research into my ancestry. When I explained the nature of my interest to the senior archivist, the latter asked the ethnic origin of those ancestors. Upon hearing that they were Irish he made two comments. "You are wasting your time because all of the Irish records were burned up in one of their civil wars years ago." As he turned to walk away he added, "You are wasting our time too, since there is nothing here about the Irish. They have been trouble wherever they went!"

At the time I was abashed, but reflection led me to the resolution to do what might be in my power to change not only that attitude, but also to do what I could to make the path of Irish genealogy easier for those who followed. Peggy Magee is doing much the same sort of thing.

The Irish must be sought on both sides of the Atlantic by their North American descendants, and in a wide variety of sources. There was a germ of truth in the offhanded remarks of that archivist. There were many customary records incinerated in Dublin during "the troubles": census returns, wills, original and duplicate Anglican registers. Other records do not exist because they were never created, such as rural Catholic Parochial registers predating 1820 or so. A consequence of this has been a brilliant display of genius by Irish genealogists. In a phrase, the Irish family historian has had to become eclectic, borrowing everywhere to augment or replace the unobtainable record. Mrs. Magee exemplifies this spirit and has taken pains to point out the necessity of casting the net wide in Irish ancestral research. It is the only system to follow if you wish to do productive investigation.

Part of the secret of Irish research is to determine three things _before_ having records in Ireland searched: the name or names of those in whom you are interested, a time context, and a geographical frame of reference. One would not consider researching abroad without knowing for whom one was looking. If that person's name was common, it will be of little use all by itself. You must obtain the names of all those, whether kin or companions, who came out of Ireland with the forebear. Among the several names may be one which is rare or localized enough to supply a clue about the location of the ancestral home in Ireland.

Headstones, census returns and quite a respectable variety of other sources can provide the approximate or exact age of the ancestor. Failing that, the work of Filby and others may enable you to find a record of immigration or passage, connected with a date. As British subjects, the Irish were often naturalized in the United States. In

Canada until the twentieth century, British
citizenship was common to Ireland and
several other provinces, hence no records
of that nature exist to help Canadians.

The critical point in seeking Irish
lines must be location. There is great
need to pinpoint a family within Ireland.
Otherwise the descendant of a farmer or
artisan, spalpeen or fisherman is apt to
waste much time and money in an often
fruitless search dedicated to finding the
right haystack in which to seek a needle.
It is that difficult, which is why new
hands at Irish genealogy ought to heed the
advice of Peggy Magee and those like her
who know what they are talking about.
Matheson's works on Irish surnames are
more useful than the family location maps
based on ownership patterns from the 1650s.
Griffith's Valuations and the Tithe
Applotment Books replace lost census
returns as locators of families. The
present book offers further suggestions.

It is an honour to be asked to write the
forward for a book compiled by a worker who
is so dedicated to Irish ancestral
research. Once, while in Cork on a visit,
I was told by the late John T. Collins that
in Irish research one must never be a
<u>bonave</u>. This, he explained, was a little
pig. His moral was clear, that we be
willing to share our information and our
leads with others. In writing this book, I
believe the author is sharing her expertise
and knowledge. For the alert reader may
this be the key to unlock some of the
secrets of his or her Irish genealogy.

-Terrence M. Punch, F.R.S.A.I.
Halifax, Nova Scotia, Canada

Starting the Search

The mention of pursuing one's ancestors in Ireland too many times is greeted with the statement, "All the records were destroyed in the fire at Four Courts." True, many records, including a large portion of census records, wills and other documents were burned. However, many records deposited in Four Court were not destroyed. The National Library of Ireland, the Genealogical Office, the Registrar General's Office, the Registry of Deeds along with many other repositories in Dublin had nary a spark near them. Take notice that there are millions of vital records, document collections, census substitutes, leases, deeds, marriage settlements, wills, estate records, parish registers, books, pedigree charts and documents of various descriptions to lead you down the path of ancestral discovery.

Genealogical research is different in Ireland, as is the case whenever you pursue your research in a different country, state or province. It is something new to the researcher but once you know what is available and where, and what years are covered by particular collections, etc., then the research can be done in an orderly and fulfilling manner.

The first step in tracing your Irish ancestor is to uncover as much information on this side of the ocean as possible. You can never have too much information on your immigrant ancestor. Often the information collected is limited to the bare vital records, which in most instances, list the ancestor's place of birth as simply, Ireland. The country of birth provides the researcher with as many clues as an ancestor's birthplace being listed as Canada or the United States without state or province recorded. The most valuable piece of information is the Irish townland and parish of his birth. You may ask why both? In many instances there is more than one townland by the same name in the same county but only one of that name in a parish. The town of Ballina in Co. Mayo appears four times and in four different parishes. This is not an isolated occurrence and many other similiar repetitions of townland names in a county could be listed.

Tracking down the name of the townland and parish may be quite easy for you but for some researchers, it can be a lifelong task. Therefore, you should be as familiar as possible with North American records and the information you can obtain from them. There might be a couple on the following list that you have not checked.

Research in America

VITAL RECORDS

These include birth, marriage and death certificates, not only for your immediate ancestor but their siblings and <u>all children</u>. Many vital records are filed in three places: at municipal, county and state or province level. Try to obtain all the documents for each event. There is also a possibility of a hospital maintaining a fourth set of records in which a place of birth might have been requested, rather than just country of birth.

NAMES OF SIBLINGS

If you have acquired the vital records as described above, you have this information at hand. Take a piece of paper and note carefully the name and date of birth of your ancestor and his siblings; then the children of each of these. Usually a pattern of naming will appear. In the Irish tradition, the first born son was named for the paternal grandfather and the second born son for the maternal grandfather. The daughters were frequently named in the same manner. One note of caution - should the first born die, the next born son would be named for the paternal grandfather. The rest of the sons and daughters usually would be named for uncles, aunts, cousins, etc. You now could have very valuable clues to the first names of your ancestor's parents that may have died on the voyage to America or stayed behind in Ireland.

LOCAL HISTORY

Know the history of the town where your ancestor settled in America. Either go to or write the local public library or the historical society of the town or county. Learn as much as you can about the people living in your ancestor's neighborhood or arriving from Ireland at the same time as your ancestor. Many times, once the Irish had settled in their new country, they would send money for relatives & friends to join them. Though your ancestor may have not reached a degree of prominence, the very friend, to whom he sent passage money, may have. Keep track of the prominent people, their surnames and any mention of their birthplace in Ireland; -- even county.

OTHERS LISTED IN VITAL RECORDS

Take careful note of those other names listed on records as they may possibly contain clues or in the future should be researched themselves. The names of godparents, witnesses at weddings or informants on death certificates may be leads to sisters' or daughters' married names, etc. Do not just extract the information on your own ancestor but keep these names in a small notebook as ready reference when searching other records.

CENSUS RECORDS

Since many other books, such as the "Handy Book" and the "Source", have elaborated on the state and federal census records available, only a few additional hints should suffice. Whenever possible have a photocopy of the census page for your records. Note carefully all of the information included on each census. While you are researching the census, check out the neighborhood - note other Irish close by. Some of those may be cousins, godparents, etc. Should these names have appeared in other records write down the information in your notebook.

CHURCH RECORDS

Through the local library or historical society, you can obtain the names of the churches in existence when the first generation Irish-Americans were born. Write to the church for the baptismal records. Many times these will include more information than a civil registration. Catholic baptismal records give the maiden name of mothers. Sometimes the two surnames (if not too common) can be a clue to the place of origin in Ireland. Should you find that the church is no longer in existence, you will have to write to an Archive or Historical Library. For Protestant records, look in a World Almanac for a Society for the denomination of your ancestor and write to them. For Catholic records, write to the Diocese or Archdiocese for the area where your ancestor resided. Catholic Archives are being set up in each Diocese. When writing to an Archive or library, inquire about any histories written on the church your ancestor attended and the cost of xerox or published copies of any histories.

<u>CEMETERIES</u>

Whenever possible go to the cemetery in person. Many tombstones show the place of birth. While you are there with your little notebook, check for the other names you have written down. If your ancestor's tombstone does not have this information inscribed, the tombstone of a godparent, etc. may have it. When writing or visiting a cemetery, inquire from the caretakers, who else might be interred in the plot, and when all interments took place as well as the purchase date of the plot. Any new name found should also be researched.

<u>LAND RECORDS</u>

Land records may or may not provide birthplace information. Your chances of obtaining land information is better prior to the famine. In eastern and central Canada, be particularly aware that many land grants were given in lieu of military pension, especially in the early 1800s. You might want to pursue military and pensions records in England. Remember also to check out the neighborhood for other names in your notebook. Civilian settlers petitioning for land grants often mentioned country or county of origin and year of arrival.

<u>NATURALIZATION</u>

In the United States, you will find three possible forms utilized in the process of natiralization depending on the state and time period.

A Declaration of Intention was required in many states after the 1850s to purchase land; previously only naturalized citizens could purchase land. The information required varies from county to county and from state to state. Declarations could have been filed in the state where your ancestor arrived from Ireland, the state where he finally settled or anywhere in between.

Petitions for Naturalization were usually filed at the county level and usually provide more information but these petitions may not be readily available.

The Naturalization papers may be a simple form signed and witnessed or a document containing the date and place of your ancestors birth, including the ship, date, and port of arrival. Information varies from county to county and state to state.

You should attempt to obtain all of these documents. Petitions may be the most difficult of the three to obtain from county court houses but are well worth the extra effort.

Canada was British North America until 1867. Irish people were British subjects and needed no naturalization there until well into the twentieth century.

PROBATE RECORDS

Wills and probate records should be pursued not only in the year of death, but many years thereafter. Many times the probate matters would not be filed until someone wanted to dispose of the land or other property. If there was no will, letters of administration would have to have been filed. Sometimes real property was settled by land deed in which several heirs jointly sold their rights to one person.

OBITUARIES

Once you have determined the date of death, get a copy of the obituary. In recent years, many of the old copies have been microfilmed and are housed in the local library or college. The obituary can give you the name of the church and the cemetery, if you do not have them. It can also provide you with the names of other relatives. Examine published indexes to newspaper vital records if these exist for the area of death.

ORGANIZATIONS

Many of our ancestors joined organizations which may still have membership records.

Many Catholics became members of the Knights of Columbus or the Ancient Order of Hibernians while non Catholics became members of the Orange Lodge, Masons, or other organizations. Check with the local library or Chamber of Commerce for the address or the World Almanac for the national headquarters. Some societies have deposited early minute books in public archives (e.g. Charitable Irish Society of Halifax, 1786 -, in Public Archives of Nova Scotia.)

Check on union membership and employment records. Remember many of the early Irish worked on the canals, while in post famine years the railroads employed thousands. Census records, obituaries, death certificates should provide many clues.

Whenever you are writing to organizations or unions, ask if the organization provided any insurance and where the records might be. Many times insurance applications required place, not just country, of birth

PASSENGER LISTS

United States ship manifests were not required to be filed until 1820, though a very limited number prior to this have surfaced. Most U.S. manifests will list the place from whence the passenger came as Ireland or even Great Britain. Before the famine you may find some passenger lists with the townland or parish lists but these are exceptional finds.

Canada did not require the filing of passenger lists until the 1860s and then only for foreign born passengers. Ancestors born in England, Scotland, Wales or Ireland were not considered foreign born. A few lists do exist -- mainly extracted from personal records of agents responsible for settlement of large tracts or Emigrant Hospital records. Local histories can provide clues as to settlements, etc.

If you know the year of arrival in North America, check a local newspaper in America and a Dublin or Belfast newpaper. Shipping companies occasionally would publish a list of passengers who had safely crossed the ocean as a means of advertising for the return passage to Ireland or for the next sailing from Ireland.

When working with a passenger to the United States, the year 1825 is very

significant.   In   this year the Erie Canal
was completed and made New York the busiest
port   in   the   U.S.   Prior   to   that year,
Philadelphia   was   the   port of destination
for most ships.

The   canals   and   rivers   provided   the
immigrants   with   inexpensive   travel   in the
U.S.   and Canada prior to the developement
of   the   railroad   systems.   If you do not
know   the   port of entry, study maps of the
rivers   and   canals to determine how he may
have   traveled   to   inland   states   and
provinces.   Many   who   settled in the U.S.
arrived   at   Canadian   ports   and   then
journeyed   through   the lakes and rivers to
the   inland states.   While many who settled
in Canada arrived in U.S. ports and went
north   by   canals   or   ocean   steamers   to
Canadian ports.

BE FLEXIBLE

Errors   in   the   spelling   of   your
ancestor's   surname should be accepted very
early   in   your   genealogical   work.   The
stronger   the   brogue,   coupled   with   an
inability   to   spell   can   lead to numerous
variations   of   the   name.   Even   if   your
ancestor   was literate, but the information
provided   orally, there is a good chance of
error.   Townlands,   parishes   and   even
counties   are   written   exactly   as   the
recorder's   ear heard them. And that, in
most   instances,   is   not the correct Irish
spelling.   The ideal records would be ones
which   were   written   out   by the immigrant
ancestor,   but   this type seems to be quite
scarce.

Some   records   which   are   highly
questionable are death certificates, census
records   and tombstones.   Give some thought

to the circumstances surrounding the record. Imagine HOW it came into being: who may have given the information and if any inaccuracies could have occurred.

Usually death certificates are only as good as the memory of the informant. Many times the date of birth is erroneously given and data on parents and place of birth omitted. More accurate information can be assumed when submitted by the parents of a small child or the spouse of the deceased. Children as informants usually do not know all the data on the deceased parent. Neighbors or other informants have even less information. The circumstances of the death of a loved one and the stress placed on the survivors, can create a lack of memory of the facts. The mother's maiden name is one of the hardest things to remember in such a situation.

Many Irish seem to have been missed in the 1850 & 1860 U.S. census reports. Many were living in violation of housing laws and the landlords were afraid to admit that they were renting the basement or some other parts of their property.

The accuracy of census reports depend on the recorder of the information and the informant. The subject of spelling errors has been previously discussed, so now we will look at age/date of birth as listed on the census.

Pretend you are a census taker - the man of the house is responding to your question of the age of the residents. He states he was born in 13, his wife in 21, and his children in 41, 44, 48, and 53. The year is 1860 and you have been going house to

house for over six hours. Your subtraction
ability possibly is not as sharp as it was
at   10 this morning when your feet were not
hurting so much. Some chance of a error?
Good possibility.

Now for the respondent to the questions
- there are also chances of error. How
many times have you been asked the age of
your children or even your own age, and had
to think about it! What if the oldest
child was answering the questions? He or
she may not know the correct age of the
parents. And let's not forget about the
women, who in reality were older then their
husbands, and never gave a straight
answer.

Many times tombstones are erected years
after the death of the ancestor. In the
ensuing years, memories of dates fade and
guesses are made. Tombstone dates should
not be accepted as accurate until verified
by other records. Do not consider any
record as carved in stone, even if it is.
Check out all possible variants and dates,
even up to 10 years in difference,
especially with only adult records
available.

The Irish in America

The first record we have of the Irish in America is in cave drawings in West Virginia. These carvings in ogham, an old Irish alphabet, prove the Irish landed around 400 A.D. For additional information, read the Saturday Evening Post, September 1984 issue

The next Irishman to grace our continent is found in the archives of Madrid. In the records of Columbus' voyage to the New World, it is stated that Patrick Maguiness was first to set foot on land. How did he get on the ship? For centuries, an Irish legend has existed that Columbus stopped in Ireland to take on additional supplies. Could he also have taken on additional crew?

If you look at the officers who accompanied Coronado on his expedition to the southwest, you will note many Irishmen but the names are spelled as a Spaniard heard them - Malconel; Murfie, Obrin, etc.

The records of Sir Walter Raleigh state that he had two Irishmen with him at

Jamestown.

This brings us up to the 1600s, and the period's unique reluctance to identify the Irish. During the 17th, 18th and early 19th century, many town records clearly state residents' place of origin as being Dublin, Cork, Londonderry, Coleraine, etc. The inaccuracies of birthplace are in the genealogical books written in the last half of the 19th century and down through a good portion of the early years of this century.

We have discussed imagining the circumstances of a record coming into being; imagine a writer in the 1850s face to face with an Irish ancestor who migrated in the 1600s or 1700s. The times put the Irish at the lowest rung of the social structure. Could there be anything worse than having an ancestor who was Irish? In good social circles, NO!

Check carefully the date of the genealogy, which you have taken as "gospel", was written. Was it between 1850 and perhaps 1930? This is the time period for a question arising in your mind as to your ancestors' nationality. One has to wonder, how many thousands of researchers have been misled by books written during the dark ages of Irish American genealogy. Not to mention the money spent in chasing phantom English connections.

Top on the list of probable Irish ancestors would be those with such very Irish first names as Patrick, Michael, Darby, etc., but also John, Thomas, Peter and many others could be Irish. To many researchers it seems unbelievable that a Smith, Logan, White, Phillips or some other English name could have resided in Ireland.

Hard to believe that William Penn became a
Quaker in Ireland and his relatives resided
in county Cork as recently as 30 years ago!
But true!

A knowledge of Irish history can be a
true awakening! English names have been in
Ireland for centuries.   And in many
instances, these English sounding names are
really anglicized versions of ancient Irish
names. Smith can be in reality MacGowan.

Some authors listed the origins of an
ancestor as birthplace unknown. Others
stated <u>probably</u> born in England. Still
others coined a phrase, and listed him as
"Scotch-Irish".

<u>"SCOTCH-IRISH"</u>

If you walk up to an Irishman in Dublin
or Belfast and inquire if he be
"Scotch-Irish", he would probably answer
that he never knew one existed! In the
area of Irish and Scottish genealogy, this
one phrase can hinder your genealogical
research more than anything else.

What definition do you give to
"Scotch-Irish"? Some which have been
discussed in the past include: an ancestor
who arrived prior to the Revolution; an
Irishman who was not Catholic; an
Ulsterman; an Irishman, whose ancestors
originated in Scotland; an Irishman whose
ancestors came from Scotland during the
Ulster plantation; anyone whose surname
starts with "Mac" or "Ma" or anyone whose
lineage cannot be traced to the clans of
Ireland.

Some use the United States Revolutionary
War period as the time for Scotch-Irish,

while others use prior to 1840 as the migration time of the Scotch-Irish. Therefore, you will find Sullivans, McCarthys, Murphys and numerous other names labeled "Scotch-Irish".

Many feel that Catholics are Irish and non-Catholics are "Scotch-Irish". Again, we must be knowledgeable of the local history of the area where the ancestor settled. Were there any Catholic churches there? If there weren't, how could he have attended a Catholic Church or have his children baptized Catholic? Quite simply, he couldn't. He would have had to choose another religion for himself and his family. Prior to the Great Famine of the 1840s, there were not very many Catholic churches in North America. Catholics and Presbyterians in the 1600s and 1700s would have choosen an Anglican or Episcopal Church last because of its ties to the Church of Ireland.

The Penal Laws, which were imposed in Ireland just after 1700, were not only against the Catholics, but opposed any religion except the Church of Ireland. All marriages that were not performed in the Church of Ireland were invalid. No one could inherit a lease of any years duration unless they were members of the Church of Ireland.

The Penal Laws were much more oppressive to Catholics than Protestants, but usually if an ancestor was not a member of the Church of Ireland, he would not affliate with the Anglican or Episcopal church on this side of the ocean. Knowledge of the conditions in Ireland around the time of an ancestor's migration is very important.

Religion does not make an Irishman. Both Dublin and Cork have had Lord Mayors who were Jewish. How could anyone say that they were not Irish?

Ulster province and the six counties which comprise Northern Ireland are not the same thing. Ulster Province consists of nine counties. Six of these counties: Armagh, Antrim, Derry, Down, Fermanagh and Tyrone compose Northern Ireland. The remaining counties: Cavan, Donegal and Monaghan are in the Republic of Ireland. An Ulsterman can come from Northern Ireland or the Republic of Ireland.

The Ulster plantation of the early 17th century was an English plan to repopulate the nine counties of Ulster Province. The large acreage was given to English "undertakers", as they were called. But many other large pieces of land were given to Irish clan chiefs, who in return promised to support the English crown. The plantation papers clearly show that the "undertakers" were to solict settlers from Scotland, but not "inland Scots". The Highlanders, at this time were called "inland Scots". So, the majority of Scots who were solicited, were lowlanders. The plantation papers outline that settlers of a lesser number of acres could be the "mere Irish". Therefore, the Ulster Plantation consisted of English, Lowlanders and the mere Irish.

The Celts arrived in Ireland before going northeast to Scotland. For centuries the Scots and the Irish spoke the same Gaelic language. The clans on both sides of the Irish Sea helped each other out in times of war, and many clans had branches or septs in both countries. The famous Stewart Clan traces its lineage to the High

Kings of Ireland. These people moved back and forth long before the Ulster Plantation. Because your ancestor has a Scottish sounding name does not necessarily mean he was a settler in Ireland during the Plantation. If the name is one of the Highland clans, he probably wasn't unless he was attached to the British army. Assuming is not part of genealogical research methods.

In the old Gaelic, all surnames beginning with MA, MC or MAC were all MAC which means son of. All of these spellings can be Irish. The O' means grandson of.

There are many surnames in Ireland that are not derived from the clans of Ireland but have been in the country for 800 years. Many are Normans, French, German, and English who through the centuries have settled in Ireland. Today in Ireland there are residents whose roots come from Japan, Viet Nam and many other counties.

If you are born in the United States or Canada, you would call yourself American or Canadian. So, if your ancestor was born in Ireland, he was Irish. To a genealogist the phrase "Scotch-Irish" is not very helpful. If you want to be more descriptive, state he was Catholic, Presbyterian, Quaker or whatever his religious denomination was. There are church registers which can be researched when this type of information is given to a genealogist.

DO NOT use the phrase "Scotch-Irish" when writing or researching in Scotland. It can send a Scotsman into a tirade. In no uncertain terms, you will be told that the only thing that is Scotch in Scotland is the whiskey! Whenever you are in

Scotland or writing to Scotland, remember your ancestors were Scots, Scotsmen or Scottish. The use of "Scotch" can mean the difference between getting help or not getting help. Using the proper terminology, will make things much easier for you in your research.

Without Going To Ireland

As previously stated, having a good knowledge of the history of Ireland for the period during which your ancestor lived, is extremely helpful. The question in genealogists' minds is "Why did he leave?". It does not make sense for you to ask a professional genealogist to answer this question, when a book on Irish history would most likely give you the answers.

What can be done on this side of the ocean, depends on where you live and whether you have access to a Mormon Library. Certainly if you know the name of the townland and parish, you can do quite a bit by mail. In the following information, you should pay particular attention to the records which have been filmed by the LDS church. You may want to rent the films or view them in Salt Lake City.

Many of the major county or local histories of Ireland and even family histories in print are only to be found at the large libraries in the U.S. and Canada. The most complete collections are to be found at Linenhall Library in Belfast or the National Library in Dublin.

If you do not know the townland or even
the county in Ireland where your ancestors
came from, the first task is to limit the
counties down to workable size. Surnames
of Ireland by Edward MacLysaght will give
you the original areas where the name
resided. A better source would be the
Matheson Report on Surnames or the name
index to the Griffith Valuations and Tithe
Applotment Books.

The Matheson Report is based on the
number of births registered in 1890 by
province but also shows the counties having
the most number of births. However, only
names having five or more births recorded
for that name were included in the report.

Though a more detailed explanation of
the Griffith's Valuations and Tithe
Applotment Books will be forthcoming, these
two important substitutes for census
records were indexed by the National
Library several years ago. These indexes,
along with the actual Valuations have been
microfilmed and are available at many large
libraries and genealogical societies. The
microfiche can also be purchased through
Magee Publications, P.O. Box 26507,
Prescott Valley, AZ 86312. You can
purchase the name indexes for all 32
counties or index and Valuations for a
particular county. The indexes will show
you where and how many people by that
surname were recorded.

Of course, you can always hire a
professional genealogist. One cannot
expect a genealogist to guarantee results.
One only knows if the information is there
AFTER researching the records. Research
in Ireland can be quite time consuming.
Waiting for documents, microfilm readers

and many other waiting periods usually can add a half to a full hour per repository. If you are going to hire someone, spend as much money as you can, not as little as you can. It is much better for a researcher to stay with a case rather than pick it up again at a later date. Many times, a researcher will be very close to the breakthrough point, only to have to stop because the client only wants four hours of research time and no more. You might think that the researcher should continue anyway but after clients not paying you for additional work, one becomes very reluctant. Be prepared to spend a minimum of $50.00 to $100.00 to start.

When you hire a genealogist to work on a Northern Ireland ancestor, pay particular attention to whether the researcher will do work in Dublin. Though the Public Record Office in Belfast has done a marvelous job in acquiring documents for their collection, and their storage vaults are perfectly controlled, there are still many things which should be searched in Dublin. Remember, there was no Public Record Office in Belfast until after 1922.

Whenever you deal directly with a researcher or repository in Ireland, certain methods will increase your chances of a reply. Genealogists in North America are accustomed to enclosing a self addressed stamped envelope with a letter. Many individuals in Ireland receive return enveloped affixed with Canadian or U.S. postage which is totally useless to them. If you do not have British or Irish postage, send an International Reply coupon for a surface reply or two coupons for air mail response. Whenever you are writing to a smaller town where the exchange of coupons for postage may not be available, enclose $1.00 in U.S. or Canadian currency.

It is always proper to enclose $10.00 whenever you are requesting a priest or minister to take his spare time to check parish registers. His primary duty is the members of his parish and some compensation for his time should be freely given with the initial request.

Patience is the keyword when dealing with the Irish. North Americans always seem to be in such a rush to the average Irishman. Time is just not that important in Ireland. The famous phrase of Scarlett O'Hara in "Gone With the Wind" , "I'll think about that tomorrow" is a typical Irish thought. It is frustrating when you are trying to do research but polite low keyed remainders are the best way to obtain your goals.

Divisions of Ireland

Whether attempting your research here or in Ireland, one must be aware of the administrative divisions of Ireland and how records may be filed, etc.

Ireland consists of four provinces: Leinster, Munster, Connacht(Connaught) and Ulster.. Carlow, Dublin, Kilkenny, Kildare, Longford, Laois (Queen's), Louth, Meath, Offaly (King's), Westmeath, Wexford and Wicklow are in the province of Leinster. Munster Province is comprised of Clare, Cork, Kerry, Limerick, Tipperary and Waterford counties. While Galway, Leitrim, Mayo, Roscommon, and Sligo are in Connacht Province. The nine counties of Ulster are Antrim, Armagh, Cavan, Derry, Donegal, Down, Fermanagh, Monaghan and Tyrone.

Dioceses are utilized by both the Catholic Church and the Church of Ireland. The boundaries are different - there being more Catholic dioceses. The utilization of dioceses is not limited to searches of parish registers. Up until the mid 1800s many legal matters were handled by the diocese administration. All probate matters, marriage license bonds, etc. were done in the local diocese based on the

Church of Ireland divisions until 1858.

The thirty-two counties of Ireland, as known today, came into being in 1606 with the creation of county Wicklow. The only exception being King's and Queen's which were returned to their old names of Offaly and Laois(Leix) after 1922. There are many different spellings of the names of the counties prior to the eighteenth century.

Ireland had a total of two hundred and seventy-three baronies. Each barony was an administrative, tax and regional division within the county. Many records which genealogists use list the barony. Knowledge of the barony is necessary in using the county books at the Registry of Deeds and helpful in other records. Baronies occasionally were located across county lines and formed part of more than one county.

There are parishes and then there are parishes in Ireland. There are civil parishes and ecclesiastical parishes. When you are dealing with civil records, state or county records, you will be using the names of the civil parishes. Church records are of the religious parish which may or may not be the same name as the civil parish. Civil parishes may extend to one or more counties. Catholic parishes are confined to the county boundaries.

The smallest administrative division in the country is the townland. There are about 64,000 townlands in Ireland. Because many townlands were named for the area and a distinguishing feature such as a ridge, hill, glen, etc., there are many townlands with the same name. Many have Irish, Old-English and English names. The use of

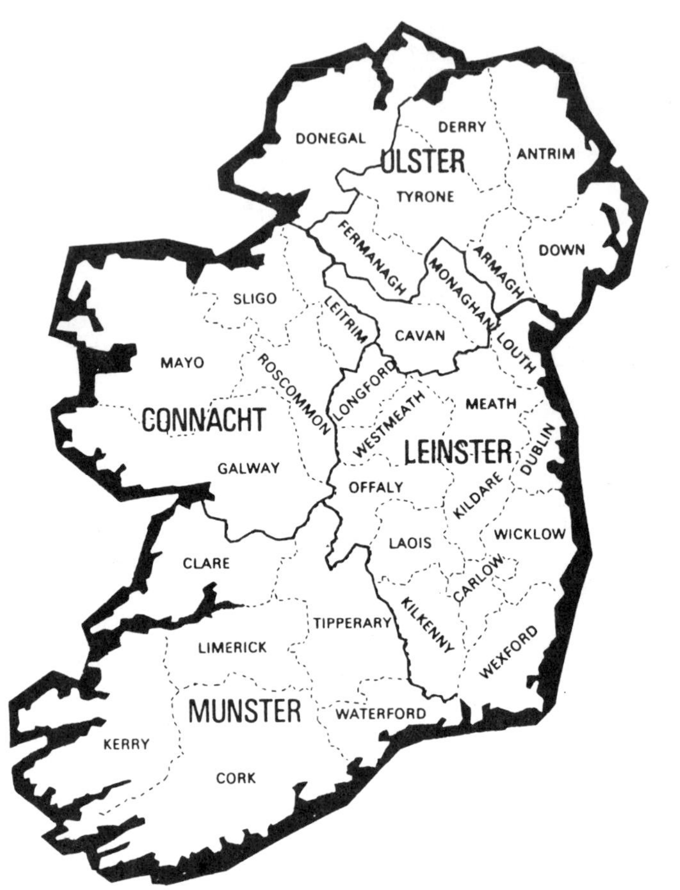

MAP OF IRELAND
showing provinces and counties

surnames in the townland names is quite common and was done to indicate the principal family or large owners in the area.

Be armed with as much knowledge as possible about the townland or county that you are researching in Ireland before you go. There is a suggested book list at the back of this book.

Primary Research Sources

<u>CIVIL RECORDS</u>

Births have been recorded in Ireland since 1864. Though the first couple years the registrations from the northwest counties seems to be less than one would expect, all records for Northern Ireland until 1922 are in Dublin and Belfast. After that, the records are in Belfast. Birth certificates list the father and mother's maiden name and place of residence.

Death records also start in 1864. The records for Northern Ireland until 1922 are both in Dublin and Belfast. Deaths after 1922 are in Belfast. Certificates show place of residence, age, and name of person present at death.

Marriage records also started in 1864 except for Protestant marriages which started in 1845. Northern Ireland records prior to 1922 are found in Dublin and held by District Registrars in each District Council Area; after 1922 at the latter. Marriage records show the names of the bride and groom, their ages, location of residence, fathers' names and occupations.

There are name index books for all three types of registrations. Most of the indexes are divided by quarters and list the registration office. You would be well advised to have a map of Ireland with you as there is usually more than one registration office per county and you may not know which registration offices are in what county.

The above indexes have been microfilmed by LDS but to obtain the certificate by mail from Dublin you must provide the year, quarter and page. The fees for certificates have been increasing over the past few years. I would suggest sending US$2.00 or Canadian $2.50 per certificate. Personal checks in US or Canadian funds are accepted. Send your orders for certificates to the Registrar General in Dublin. The address is included in the chapter on Repositories.

Admission to the General Register Office in Belfast is by appointment only through the Registrar. Copies of certificates may be obtained by mail for US$5.50 or Canadian $7.00 which includes a five year search. The District of death is needed to research death certificates. The address is in the list of Repositories.

The indexes to Marriage License Bonds are in the Public Record Office in Dublin (PROI) listed by diocese and start in 1623 or later depending on the diocese. Some indexes have been published (e.g. Cork, Cloyne, Ross).

Marriage Settlements were frequently recorded and are to be found among the records of the Registry of Deeds. See the following on Land Records.

<u>HAYES</u> <u>BOOKS</u>

In the upcoming discussion of sources, the mention of the Hayes books will occur several times. Actually, Dr. Richard Hayes, formerly of the National Library of Ireland, put together many volumes called Manuscript Sources for the History of Irish Civilization. There is a set of books for places, one for subjects, one for persons, and one for dates. There is also a series of books for material found in periodicals based on the same catagories. A supplement was printed for both manuscripts and periodicals. One volume was written on manuscripts in the Irish language. Since the supplements, additional materials have been indexed on card files in the manuscript room of the National Library in Dublin. The books and index cards list manuscripts and periodicals which contain information on Ireland and where the material is housed in 678 libraries in 30 countries and in over 600 private collections.

These books should be consulted for each surname to see if there might be a collection for the name. In researching a particular townland, you turn to the county, then check barony, parish (civil and religious) and then the townland. The listing can lead to many manuscripts not listed in Irish research manuals. As other catagories of research sources are discussed, you will be reminded to check the Hayes books. Many of the larger libraries in the United States and Canada have a set of Hayes books. It would be beneficial to you to locate a set close to your home.

CENSUS RECORDS

Because of the fire in Four Courts in 1922, many people are surprised to learn that the 1901 census for all of Ireland is still in existence. It is not indexed and is housed at PROI in Dublin. The census is filed by baronies within each county. With only the name of the county of birth, it can take many hours to research an entire county, especially the heavily populated counties, such as Cork. The 1911 census is also complete and can be found at PROI, Dublin and is filed as outlined for the 1901 census. All census records for the Republic and Northern Ireland prior to 1922 are in Dublin.

Working backwards, as one always does in genealogy, the 1871 and 1861 census records were destroyed. not by the fire, but by the order of the government. To the best of anyone's knowledge, the decision not to preserve the information was made by the government.

Most of the 1851 census was destoyed in the fire. However, some reports for parishes in Co. Antrim and Co. Cork escaped the fire, as well as one townland in Co. Fermanagh. These records are at PROI and have been microfilmed.

The only surviving parish census of 1841 is Killeshandra, Co. Cavan. This is at PROI as well as having been microfilmed. Forty-one of the forty-eight parishes of Co. Derry are the only remains of the 1831 census. They are also at PROI and have been microfilmed.

For the 1821 census, the following remain: 1 parish in Co. Armagh, 16 parishes in Co. Cavan, 2 baronies of Co. Galway, a good portion of 1 parish in Co. Fermanagh, 9 parishes of Offaly (King's Co.) and 19 parishes of Co. Meath. All of these are at the PROI and have been microfilmed. Copies of some census records, made by researchers prior to 1922, also exist, either in manuscript or published in genealogical journals.

Between 1659 and 1821 there are many local, parish and diocese censuses, notably the 1766 "religious census". The manuscript numbers are noted in the Hayes books.

The Census of Ireland circa 1659 compiled by Sir William Petty was published by the Irish Manuscripts Commission in 1939. It lists only those with title to lands and total number of English and Irish in each townland. The counties of Cavan, Galway, Mayo, Tyrone and Wicklow have not survived. Only three baronies for Co. Meath are included.

The Civil Survey of Ireland was done 1654-1656 by Sir William Petty. This survey lists the then landlords of the townlands as well as the former owners prior to Cromwell. Some of these surveys by county have been published by the Irish Manuscripts Commission. The remainder are to be found at PROI. They are called the Books of Survey and Distribution.

<u>CENSUS</u> <u>SUBSTITUTES</u>

Among the many substitutes are Freeholders lists which were completed at various times in the counties. Also you can find applications to bear firearms and a variety of other documents listed in the Hayes Books. The largest amount of manuscripts will be found at PROI, PRONI and the National Library in Dublin. Many of these were published in entirety as books, while others are to be found in local history books which are not housed in the manuscript collection of the National Library, but rather in the main body of the library and available during opening hours.

The two most accepted substitutes for the census are the Griffith Primary Valuations (PV) and the Tithe Applotment Books (TAB).

An Index to surnames contained in the PV and TAB has previously been discussed. The Name Index lists the number of times the name appears by Barony for the PV but does not show the number of times the name appears in TAB. Once you have ascertained what baronies the name appears in, then you check each parish in the barony for the name.

When researching the PV, once you have the information, you search the original valuations. The information on the PV contains the occupant, the name of the immediate lessor, description of holdings – house, land, garden, yard, etc, value of land, buildings and combined value of land and buildings.

The PV will give you the name of the townland. Some other pertinent information should be recorded by you, not just the townland and name. Look closely at the description of the holdings. Is a house included? Many times an ancestor had land which he tilled but did not live on it. Look for others of the same name in the parish who could be relatives with whom he was living.

Many times the name of the lessor is not recorded by the genealogist but should be, along with any large land lessors in the parish. Many of these land owners' estate records are in either of the PROs and can provide much information on the tenants. The land owners names should be checked in the Hayes books to determine the location of the documents.

The Tithe Applotment Books (TAB) for the 26 counties of the Republic are at the PROI and microfilmed copies of all 32 counties are at the National Library of Ireland in Dublin. The originals for the Northern Ireland counties are in PRONI.

The usual information found on the TAB includes townland, occupier and value of the land. It may also contain the amount of tithe assessed. The TAB are handwritten whereas the PV are mostly in printed form. Many times there are several books per parish. The LDS did microfilm TAB but overlooked some books, not realizing there could be more than 1 book per parish.

The TAB ONLY lists rural dwellers, not city residents. It covers 1823-1837 and the survey was started south of Dublin and works its way westward and then to the north and east back down to County Dublin.

The Green Sheets, as they are commonly referred to by genealogists, are pension applications from 1908. When the pension law was enacted and residents in Ireland, Scotland, Wales and England applied, the birth information that was submitted was verified with census records. At that time, the 1851, 1841 and previous census records were still intact. When verifying the information, the parents and other siblings were extracted and recorded on the

PUBLIC RECORD OFFICE OF NORTHERN IRELAND
in Belfast

(Photograph compliments of the Northern Ireland Tourist Board)

Green Sheets from one or more censuses. Though your immigrant in 1908 may not have resided in Great Britain and applied for a pension, a brother or sister, remaining on the other side of the Atlantic may have applied.

The extracted information on the Green Sheets has not been indexed and is filed by parish, barony and county at PROI.

<u>INDEX CARD FILES</u>

The Public Record Offices in Belfast and
Dublin and the Genealogical Office in
Dublin all have index card files. The
Genealogical Office's card files consist of
will extracts as well as other manuscripts
in their possession. The Public Record
Office in Dublin maintains several index
card files which provide extracts from some
material burned in 1922. The Public
Record Office in Belfast has the largest
number of index cards of the three
repositories, -- noting the document
numbers and type of information. All the
index card files can provide you with
information on your ancestor or suggest
document collections which you should
persue.

The newest index card files compiled are
at the National Library. One file is by
county and barony; another file is by
surname and the third is estate records by
surnames. Each card refers to many volumes
housed directly above the card files.
These volumes contain extracts of wills
contained in the Irish Land Commission -
mostly nineteenth century but some as early
as seventeenth century. The notations
listed in the volumes, i.e. E.C. 7063. Box
2985, should be pursued at the Land
Commission's Archives at 24, Upper Merrion
Street, Dublin, which is a few blocks from
the National Library. At the author's last
visit, there were no photocoping machines
available on the premises. Allow adequate
time for handcopying the documents.

CHURCH RECORDS

Roman Catholic registers for all 32 counties have been microfilmed and are at the National Library of Ireland in Dublin. Some dioceses are closed to public viewing. That does not mean that you can't find your ancestors' baptismal record but researching the registers requires written permission from the local priest or the bishop. You may also view the register in the local parish church.

The Church of Ireland registers which were in Four Courts on the day of the fire, were destroyed. However, copies of almost 60% of these registers have been located in local custody. Microfilmed copies are to be found at both Public Record Offices, and the National Library. Many local churches have the original registers. Every Protestant ancestor should be researched in these registers.

Presbyterian records are at the Public Record Offices, the Presbyterian Historical Library in Belfast or in local custody.

The Society of Friends (Quakers) maintains a library in Dublin. The records are excellent back to the 1600s. Many Quaker records are also to be found in local custody.

Many Irishmen over the centuries have belonged to various demoninations. A check of the Hayes books for county and denomination can help you locate the registers.

Thom's Directories, which we will discuss shortly, lists the parishes or meeting houses for each denomination and their ministers or priests. Many times the register will be found among the document collection of the minister.

Whenever you are researching Protestants of any demonination, the registers of the Chruch of Ireland should be consulted. In order to comply with the law, marraiges, etc. had to registered with the Chruch of Ireland. Frequently, the baptisms and marriages will be found in the registers of two churches.

LAND RECORDS

The documents recorded at the Registry of Deeds in Dublin include deeds, leases, marriage settlements, business transactions and wills; - the records date back to 1708. Though non-Catholics outnumber Catholics in earlier records, these memorials, as they are called, can produce several generations through the use of the various types of volumes.

First, the name indexes of Grantors ONLY should be checked for the ten year period circa an ancestor's migration. Many times a lease or another type of sale was necessary to provide passage to a new residence. It may have transpired prior to departure or have been left to a relative or friend remaining in Ireland to transact after his departure. This type of record is more likely prior to the famine or later in the 19th century. The lessors found on the PV should also be checked for many decades prior to year of the PV noting any record where your ancestor's surname is listed as Grantee.

The Name Indexes will provide Volume (or year), page and memorial number which refer to the Day Books. In 1985 the Registry of Deeds commenced charging a fee for searching the Name Indexes.

The Day Books give a <u>condensed</u> version of the actual memorial. The Day Books' version many times refer to a previous memorial which should also be researched. Whenever you read a memorial in a Day Book which ties into your lineage, obtain a copy of the original which is kept in the vault at the Registry of Deeds. You may also obtain copies through the mail. They accept US or Canadian personal checks. I would suggest US$2.00 or $2.50 in Canadian funds.

The third set of books is known as the County Books. However, some of the volumes are just for large corporation cities – Dublin, Londonderry, Belfast, etc. When working in the County Books, you must know the townland and barony of your ancestor as most volumes list memorials by barony, subdivided by alphabetical listing for townlands. Through the County Books, one is able to find memorials relating to a particular townland and trace large estate tenants through many generations.

Though your ancestor was Catholic in Ireland, he probably leased his land from a non-Catholic and the lease may be at the Registry of Deeds. The genealogical results which one can extract from the Registry of Deeds far outweigh the time spent.

The LDS has microfilmed the Name Indexes, Day Books and County Books but <u>has not microfilmed</u> the original memorials in the vault.

Various types of land records including deeds and commerical leases can be found in both PROs and the National Library of Ireland. The manuscript numbers and document numbers will be found in the Hayes Books. Descriptions of document collections are noted in "Irish and Scotch-Irish Ancestral Research" by Margaret Dickson Falley. This two volume work includes the Deputy Keeper's Report which details the collection. Prior to spending the time of researching the collection, read the Deputy Keeper's Report to see if the years and locale warrant the time of reading each and every item in the collection. However, if you decide not to research the collection, at this time, get a copy of the Keeper's Report for your files.

PLANTATION RECORDS

Usually, the word Plantation is associated with the re-population of Ulster Province, which was touched on very lightly in a previous chapter. Plantation and settlement were words employed by the English to describe re-distributing the land from the hands of the Irish into the possession of English Protestants over more than 150 years.

It has been stated many times that a little knowledge is a dangerous thing. However, in genealogy, especially in Irish genealogy, no knowledge of history is downright foolhardy! Selecting source material for research entails some knowledge of how and when the documents came into being, what information they contain and then deciding if they can relate to your ancestor.

As brief as this little sojourn into Irish history may be, hopefully it will stimulate your interest in learning more about the Emerald Isle.

Standing in the passage way at Newgrange, one reflects on who might have built these large tombs constructed of massive slabs of rock, centuries before the pyramids in Egypt. Then seeing the Book of Kells in Trinity College Library, the awe of the beautifully illustrated Bible dating back 1200 years turns to the envitable question. "Why didn't I hear about these things in European History?" Perhaps because Ireland never became part of the Roman Empire but instead maintained its clans based on Gaelic Brehon laws. Under their system, all property belonged to all the members of the clan. The high kings were called upon to settle disputes among the clans and in some instances a game of chess decided the disagreement.

The Irish churches maintained an independence from Rome by installing their own bishops. The monastic life and scholarly achievements were unexcelled in Europe. Ireland was the educational seat of Europe. Though these centers were destroyed by the Danes in the ninth century, the ruins are visible in Glendalough, Clonmacnoise and other places. The Danes raided the east coast of Ireland and their presence is recalled by towns and cities, e.g. Wexford and Waterford. The word ford is derived from fjord.

After two hundred years the Scandinivan settlement Dublin, and other coastal towns were returned to the Irish after Brian Boru's victory in the eleventh century.

During the centuries of the clans, each
clan had its own historian who maintained
and recorded the local genealogies which
provided the information for each clan
chieftain and local ruler. Hundreds of
these ancient documents have survived and
many have been translated. The best known
is the Annals of the Four Masters.

A local dispute between two clan chiefs
lead to a plea for assistance being issued
to the Normans leaders in England. Henry
II sent mostly Normans, then dwelling in
Wales, and some English to Ireland. They
were rewarded with large parcels of land.
The hope that these Normans and Old-English
would suppress the Irish Brehon laws was
shattered as the invaders became "more
Irish than the Irish" by becoming Gaelic
speakers and dressing and living in the
Irish fashion. Only about a 60 square mile
area from Dublin to the west and south,
known as the English Pale remained loyal to
the Crown.

During the reign of Henry VIII, the
first English monarch to be called King of
Ireland, much land which was previously
connected to abbeys and monasteries was
seized as the Church of Ireland, tailored
after the Church of England, was declared
the official religion of Ireland.

Henry VIII and Edward VI, due to
rebellion on the part of the Irish
chieftains and the Anglo-Normans who
refused to surrender their lands to the
Crown, obtained the lands by declaring the
rebels guilty of treason. Some were later
pardoned. The Calendar of Patents and
Fiants show the owners of the forfeited
lands, the new English owners and those
pardoned, mostly in Counties Offaly and
Leix.

The natives of Leix and Offaly were removed to western areas during the reign of Queen Mary and the lands replanted with 160 English settlers. It was during this period that the counties were renamed King's (Offaly) and Queen's (Leix). The Patents and Fiants show former owners, and English settlers as well as those granted pardons during the period.

Under Queen Elizabeth almost 575,000 acres were declared subject to confiscation in Counties Cork, Limerick, Kerry and Waterford. Details of owners and subsequent English settlers are to be found in the Carew Manuscripts and the Patents and Fiants of Elizabeth I which are found in the PROI and the National Library.

Strafford's survey during this reign provide similiar information on County Clare and the province of Connaught, though these lands were not forfeited to the Crown.

When over 100 chieftains in Ulster went into exile on the Continent, James I confiscated all the lands of Cos. Armagh, Cavan, Derry, Donegal, Fermanagh and Tyrone. Thus began the "Plantation of Ulster" consisting of 500,000 acres. Counties Antrim and Down were partly retained by the native chieftains or replanted mostly with Scottish Presbyterians by James I. The London Guilds were responsible for the plantations of the towns of Londonderry and Coleraine. State Papers, Patents of James I and many local, county and Diocese histories contain lists of settlers.

The documents relating to Charles I's reign and prior years are supplemented by the Lodge Manuscripts in the PROI.

The years 1640-1703 produced forfeitures under Cromwell, reclaiming by "Innocents" under Charles II as well as forfeitures of the Cromwell Settlements. Under Cromwell 11 million acres were confiscated to settle debts of the Commonwealth. Those classified as guilty and subject to forfeiture included Catholics and non-Catholics in the Provinces of Leinster, Munster and Ulster who were transplanted to the province of Connaught. They settled on lands previously owned by old Anglo-Norman or Old English families who had remained Roman Catholics. The forfeited lands in Counties Antrim, Armagh, Down, King's, Limerick, Meath, Queen's, Tipperary, Waterford and Westmeath were divided between Adventurers, Englishmen who purchased subscriptions to land to be provided by future confiscation, and soldiers. All of County Louth, with the exception of the barony of Ardee, was reserved for the army. Lands were also reserved for the army in the counties of Cavan, Derry, Fermanagh, Kerry, Kilkenny, Mayo, Monaghan, Sligo, Tyrone and Wexford. Lands in Counties Donegal, Leitrim, Longford, and Wicklow were reserved for officers who served under Cromwell

Numerous documents for the reign of Charles I are listed in the Hayes Books. These provide information on the suspension of the Act of Settlement under Cromwell, the resettlement of those transplanted to Connaught, lists of those who were loyal to the Crown, Innocents, etc.

During the 17th century, there was much immigration and emigration of Scots, mostly Presbyterians in Ireland. At various times it would be more advantageous to reside in Scotland while at other times, conditions were more favorable in Ireland. The counties of Antrim and Down, due to their close proximity to Scotland, were the most popular destinations for migrating Scots.

The war between James II and his son-in-law, William of Orange, is commonly referred to as the Williamite - Jacobite war. The defeat of the Jacobites at the Battle of the Boyne lead to another period of confiscation of property. This time the defeated followers of James had their lands seized. Claims and forfeitures were heard by the Chichester House Trustees. The proceedings of the hearings and judgments are housed at the PROI and National Library in Dublin where several other manuscripts relating to this period are to be found.

The sales of 1703 of properties confiscated under William of Orange bring us to the opening of the Registry of Deeds in 1708 whose documents have been previously discussed.

ESTATE RECORDS

In America, the term, "Estate", usually is associated with probate matters. In Ireland, an Estate refers to land. The documents in estate records are quite varied. Many of the large estate owners were absentee landowners who left the operation of the estate to an agent. The reports of these agents comprise many of the records. Some estate records include maps with records of the dates and grantees of tenant leases. Other documents could include the actual leases and yearly account books listing rental payments. Some of the account books contain almost daily records of the tenants including deaths, marriages, births and forfeitures

FOUR COURTS
in Dublin, Ireland which houses the Public Record Office
of the Republic of Ireland

(Photograph compliments of Bord Failte)

of   leases.   The   National   Library   of
Ireland,   the Genealogical Office in Dublin
and   both Public Record Offices have estate
records.

In post famine years   many large estates
were   sold   at   auction.   In many instances
advertisements   for   the   sale   listed   the
tenants   and   length   of   lease.   Quite
frequently   tenants   are   listed as "gone to
America".

<u>FAMILY GENEALOGY BOOKS</u>

There have been thousands of books written on individual families. The catalogs at the National Library and the Linenhall Library should be consulted. The most recent additions will be found in the card catalog at the National Library. Dr. Edward MacLysaght compiled a Bibliography for Irish Families which originally was an Appendix to the earlier editions of <u>Surnames of Ireland</u> but now is a separate publication. The largest collection of Family Genealogy Books is at the National Library of Ireland. The next largest collection is at Linenhall Library in Belfast. But many privately printed books at found at local libraries or various college libraries.

<u>LOCAL HISTORIES</u>

Listings of local history books are to be found in the catalogs of the libraries listed above. It is important to check under the county, barony, parish and townland. Magee Publications has published a Bibliography of Genealogical Sources for the Counties of Northern Ireland and another for the counties of the Republic of Ireland which include county, diocese, and town histories. The National Library in Dublin and Linenhall Library have the most complete collections but local libraries and museums often have a privately printed book.

During the past fifteen years, a series of booklets has been published by the Ulster Architectural Heritage Society. These numerous publications deal with many small towns in Northern Ireland as well as Cavan, Donegal and Monaghan and the architecture of the area. Many old pictures, drawings as well as pictures of the area as it looks now are included. The history of old buildings are included along with the background of the town. The reference notes are very helpful tools for locating other histories on the area. Many of these booklets are still in print and can be obtained from the society at 181A Stranmills Road, Belfast, Northern Ireland.

WILLS

The second most important loss in the fire at Four Courts in 1922 was wills prior to 1904 which were housed at the Principal Registry (Four Courts), Dublin. In the ensuing years, both Public Record Offices, with the assistance of legal firms and historically minded individuals, have been replacing copies of the lost documents.

Wills from the 12th century until the Reformation in 1536 are contained in the Calendars of Patents and translations from the original Latin, French or Gaelic are to be found in numerous repositories in Dublin. Most of the wills of this era are of persons having large estates.

After the Reformation probate matters were handled on a diocese level and anyone possessing more than five pounds sterling in another Diocese, had to have his will proved or administration granted in the Prerogative Court. Therefore a small tenant farmer who resided on or close to the borderline, may have had to conform with this law.

Sir William Betham made abstracts of 37,000 wills and 5,000 Grants of Adminstrations from 1536-1800 prior to the Four Courts fire. The 241 notebooks are at the PROI. Sir William also prepared 39 volumes of "Will Pedigrees" based on the abstracts. These volumes are at the Genealogical Office in Dublin. Sir Bernard Burke, who succeeded Sir William as Ulster King of Arms, had the "Will Pedigrees" copied for his personal use. This set of 42 volumes was purchased by PRONI.

The Indexes to Wills, which survived the fire are at the PROI by Diocese with entries back to 1500s.

In 1857, probate matters were transfered to the Civil Courts. Starting in 1858 an annual Calendar to Wills and Administrations was printed. These volumes are in the reading room PROI. Even if your ancestor migrated prior to 1858, these volumes are a must for Irish researchers as emigrated relatives residing throughout the world are listed and many times the probate was started 20-30 years after death. PRONI has a similar set but limited to the District Registries of Armagh, Belfast and Londonderry.

The Registry of Deeds has many wills among its Memorials, The wills 1708-1785 were extracted by P. Beryl Eustace and published in two volumes by the Irish Manuscripts Commission, 1954-1956, recently the third volume in the series was published by the same publisher. Also the Irish Manuscripts Commission published a volume of Quaker wills. <u>Guide to Copies &</u> <u>Abstracts of Irish Wills</u> by Rev. Wallace Clare is another good book. Analecta

Hibernica, No. 17, published by the Irish Manuscripts Commission, contains 200 pages devoted to an Index of wills housed in the Genealogical Office. Many genealogical societies and public libraries have these books.

Extracts from wills at the Irish Land Commission have been discussed under Index Card Files.

Space does not permit listing all possible research materials available. For a more in depth study of Wills and Administrations see Margaret Falley's books or Irish Genealogy: A Record Finder.

NEWSPAPERS AND MAGAZINES

The earliest newspaper of genealogical importance in Northern Ireland is the Belfast Newsletter which commenced publication in 1737. The birth, marriage and death notices are being indexed at Linenhall Library. The indexing will be completed through 1850.

Various newspapers in Ireland appeared in the eighteenth century, mostly in Dublin. However many of the larger cities also had newspapers during this period.

The nineteenth century saw the birth of many new newspapers throughout Ireland. The largest collection of newspapers is at the British Library, National Library, Linenhall Library, Trinity College and numerous local libraries and colleges.

The birth information is usually scanty, usually limited to the date and sex of the child. Marriage and death notices provide more useful genealogical information. Most notices are limited to prominent people or exceptional commoners who lived to a ripe old age, etc.

Advertisements and news also provide extraordinary information for genealogists. Many ads show the change of ownership of businesses, new businesses, auctions due to death or bankruptcy. Miscellaneous items include passenger lists, electors, linen drapers, etc. Though this type is more likely to be found in the smaller newspaper. The Dublin and Belfast papers were more national in scope and death notices from all counties are to be found.

Irish Genealogy: A Record Finder has devoted an entire chapter to newspapers which provides dates of publication for the major cities.

The Hibernian Magazine and Anthologia Hibernica have been indexed. Over 13,000 items are contained in Irish Marriages by Henry Farrar. Occasionaly copies of these magazines are available for purchase in used book stores in Ireland or the United Kingdom.

There are many genealogical and historical periodicals printed in the United States, Ireland, England and Northern Ireland. But in your quest for information, include historical and archeological journals. The Falley books include a list of periodicals and many new ones have started in the 20 years since her books were written.

In 1984, while installing a new heating system in the National Library, several boxes were found containing index cards in

precise alphabetical order of all death
notices which appeared in Hibernian
Magazine. The complete file is being
microfilmed and will be available in the
near future.

DIRECTORIES

Among the hundreds of directories are
town, county and professional directories
which start in 1751. Some of the
publishers are Slator, Lucas, Pigot and
Thom. The types of residents will vary but
most town directories list merchants and
tradesmen

The most used is Thom's Irish Almanac
and Official Directory. The 1845
Directory, which was the second year of
publication, provides the following lists:

* Irish Representative Peers
* Irish Members of the House of Com-
  mons
* Orders of Knighthood
* Irish Peerage
* Baronets of Ireland
* Chief Government Officers
* Governments Departments & Officials
* Graduates of Medical University of
  Dublin
* Those Authorized to Practice Mid-
  wifery
* Physicians & Surgeons Practicing in
  Dublin
* Members of the Royal Irish Academy
* Members of many organizations & soci-
  eties
* Ecclesiatical Directory for the Esta-
  blished Church, Roman Catholic, Pres-
  byterian Church, Reformed Presbyter-
  ian, Congregational & Methodist
  Churches

* Barristers & Solicitors
* Commissioners of Affidavits
* Bank Managers
* Postmasters (12 pages)
* A directory for each county listing magistrates, county officers, stamp distributors. militia staff, etc.
* A directory of each borough listing aldermen, town concellors, custom house officials, ship & insurance brokers, newspaper proprietors & editors, etc.
* Benevolent & charitable institutions
* Directories of canal, railway & steam packet companies
* Nobility, Gentry, Merchants & Traders, Public Offices, etc., in the City of Dublin & Vicinity in 1845 (132 pgs)
* Trades Directory
* Lists of Streets and parish and ward
* Officers in Navy, Army & Coast Guard
* County Inspectors of Constabulary Force
* Revenue Police

The wealth of genealogical information provided in Thom's Directories for Dublin as well as the entire country is too frequently overlooked by researchers. The above should place this source as a must in future research plans. Thom's and other directories are found at both PROs, National Library, Linenhall Library, local libraries and colleges.

LINEAGES

Lineages, often extending back hundreds of years will be found in family genealogy books or manuscripts. The card catalog at

the National Library and Linenhall Library
and the Hayes books can lead you to the
book or manuscript. Many lineages were
submitted upon application for a coat of
arms and are in the Genealogical Office in
Dublin. Most of those are also on
microfilm at the National Library. The
index card at both PROs contain listings of
many lineages.

MILITARY RECORDS AND MUSTER ROLLS

Most military records are housed in
London at the PRO and Guildhall Library
depending on the branch of service. The
pension records are an excellent source for
eastern and central Canadian ancestors who
migrated in the early 1800s.

As discussed in the chapter on
directories, officers were listed in these
books. The date series of the Hayes Books
as well as the Subject series should be
consulted. Use the years of possible
military service to locate pertinent
manuscripts relating to Yeomen lists, etc.
The name of any particular military action,
name of war, military records, a particular
branch of service, etc. Being acquainted
with military history, is an asset. All
possibilities should be checked. The same
list should be used for the catalogs in the
National Library and Linenhall Library.
The PRO in Belfast has a separate card file
for military records. The catalogs at the
PRO in Belfast which are bound in brown
should be consulted as they contain
government records.

If you are pursuing an ancestor who was
in the Battle of the Boyne, you would check
in the Hayes books Date series around 1689,

all of the categories as listed above in the Subject series and in the Person series under King James II and King William of Orange depending on which side he fought. Using your imagination is the key.

In the past, usually the landed gentry would purchase a commission in a branch of service for the second or third born son. The eldest was always in line for the title or the lands and subsequent sons would be furnished a Church of Ireland parish or commission depending on the wealth of the family. If your ancestor was an officer, check out the landed gentry and ministers in the time period if the surname is not too common, as you will probably find a brother.

Local histories which have previously been discussed are a good source for muster lists.

<u>GRAVESTONE INSCRIPTIONS</u>

In the United States and Canada, most gravestones list the name of the person, year of birth and year of death. In Ireland, thank heaven for their gift of gab, which carries over to gravestones. Though the date of birth usually is not recorded on the stone, the month, day and year of death usually is found along with age at death. The maiden name of the wives is usually found as Mary O'Carroll alias O'Brennan. The name of the deceased father and mother might also be listed.

One intriguing feature of Irish gravestones is the common occurrence of inscriptions for sons and daughters or other family members who are not buried in Ireland. In almost every graveyard in

Ireland inscriptions are found which list someone who died in New York, Canada, etc.

Old Abbeys, Friaries, etc. are, even today, favorite burial spots for Protesants and Catholics. Many inscriptions are still legible after 300 years or more. Markers placed inside the churches usually remain years after the elements have taken their toll on the outdoor stones. But those inside the churches are usually for the nobility or famous persons.

It is not unusual to find Catholics buried in Protestant graveyards. It is unusual to find Protestant in Catholic graveyards unless it is an Abbey, etc.

There are many devoted genealogists in Ireland who faithfully record gravestone inscriptions. Some of this information is readily available on this side of the ocean and many only available in Ireland.

Brian Cantwell, who lives in Co. Wicklow, is one of those devoted inscription recorders. He completed all the graveyards in Co. Wicklow and is now working on Co. Wexford. His many volumes are housed in the PRO in Dublin, the National Library, as well as local libraries in Wicklow.

Dr. R.S.J. Clarke has completed 18 volumes on Co. Down, one on Belfast and 2 more on Co. Antrim. There are at least 2 more in preparation. This series has been published by the Ulster Historical Foundation. Thanks to a Youth Scheme to employ some of the young people in Northern Ireland, the gravestone inscriptions are being matched when possible with the Wills and Administration books. The Youth Scheme is also making possible the recording of graveyards throughout Northern Ireland which will also be available in the coming years through the Ulster Historical Foundation.

The Journals of the Association for Preservation of the Memorials of the Dead in Ireland and its successor, Journals of the Irish Memorial Association contain thousands of inscriptions in the numerous volumes. Because these journals were published as early as 1888, some of the gravestones are no longer legible.

Many genealogical periodicals printed in the United States, Ireland and England frequently publish inscriptions which have been contributed. The Hayes books, periodical series under county and townland should be consulted.

Occasionally, parish church histories will contain gravestone inscriptions.

BURIAL RECORDS

Burial records are found in parish registers of the Church of Ireland. Occasionally burials are listed in Roman Catholic records but it was not the common practice. Since most protestants were buried in a Church of Ireland graveyard, the registers should be searched for every Protestant ancestor.

The Genealogical Office has funeral certificates which contain much genealogical information. The filing of these certificates was done by members of the aristocracy and are of little use when one is working on a tenant farmer.

DEPUTY KEEPER'S REPORTS

The Deputy Keeper's Reports are simply a report to the government by the Deputy Keeper of Records on new manuscripts and document collections acquired since the last report. Many of the collections of genealogical interest are discussed in the Falley books. The Reports for the Republic of Ireland are found in the PRO, Dublin and the National Library. They have been microfilmed and are available through Magee Publications, P.O. Box 26507, Prescott Valley, AZ 86312. The appendices to these Reports contain indexes to wills and marriage license bonds totaling thousands of pages.

The Reports for Northern Ireland are at the PRO in Belfast. The index card files should be consulted as the manuscript numbers as stated in the Reports may have been changed.

IRISH MANUSCRIPTS COMMISSION

This Commission publishes a periodical entitled Analecta Hibernica. In the almost 60 years history of the Commission, 29 issues of AH have been published. The genealogical data contained in the periodical are described in the Falley books and Irish Genealogy: A Record Finder.

Many books have been published by the Commission and many are still available at their original price. This author purchased a hard bound book in 1984 for approximately $1.50. The latest books are Admission Papers of the Kings Inn and the

LINENHALL LIBRARY
in Belfast, Northern Ireland

(Photograph compliments of the Northern Ireland Tourist Board)

third volume of Registry of Deeds Abstracts of Wills.

Send a letter requesting a list of books by the Irish Manuscripts Commission that are available to Government Publications, Third Floor, St. Martin's House, Waterloo Road, Dublin 4, Ireland.

Publications of the Irish Manuscripts Commission are sold by the Government Stationery Office on Molesworth St., Dublin near Dawson St; but walk in business only. Mail orders must be sent to St. Martin's House.

Before You Leave

Before you make any plans for visiting Ireland contact the Irish Tourist Board, 757 Third Ave., New York, NY 10017 and Northern Ireland Tourist Board, 40 West 57th St., New York, NY 10019. Besides asking for brochures, maps, etc. inquire about bank holidays. There is no greater obstacle to research then finding upon your arrival that the repositories are closed for a bank holiday.

Plan your research prior to departure allowing adequate time for manuscripts and books which will be uncovered when you consult the Hayes books and card catalogues and index card files. Read over the suggested reading list in this book and acquire as many of the books as possible. Keeping in mind the time frame in which you will be working, make a list for each repository for everything you should research.

If you plan researching Catholic parish registers, at this time, the dioceses of Ardagh, Cloyne, Down & Connor, Galway, Kerry and Limerick are closed. At least two months prior to departure, you should write to the parish priest or bishop for written permission to view these registers on microfilm at the National Library. A written request accompanied by 2 International Reply Coupons, sent to the National Library will provide the name of the local priest from the current Catholic Directory.

Two other things you can do several months before you leave are contact the editors of a local newspaper in Ireland asking that anyone having knowledge of the family contact you. List your ancestor's name, birth data and probable year of migration.

Go to the nearest library and consult the phone books for Ireland. If the name you are researching is not too common, contact everyone with that surname in the country. If a common name, just write to those in the county from which your ancestor departed. In your letters list the information you have on your ancestor and ask if they have any knowledge of this family.

During my nine trips to Ireland, there is always an American or Canadian in the National Library who only has a few hours to find the townland where their ancestor lived and usually is impatient with the system of records in Ireland. As a researcher, I constantly hear stories of the lack of help received from the employees of the various repositories. This writer has always found the civil servants in Ireland go out of their way to find obscure documents and help in every way possible.

The key to a good relationship rests with the visitor. One must realize that

the repositories were not built just for
genealogists. Thousands of writers,
students, historians, etc. use the
libraries and PROs and are entitled to ask
questions of the employees. Every country
has its own system and rules with which you
have to work. First go through the card
files, catalogs, Hayes books to find
manscript numbers, call numbers for books.
If this fails to produce leads, then with a
big smile, after waiting your turn, ask for
assistance. Remember a "please and thank
you" should accompany every request. When
you talk, unless you have a brogue, the
Irish know you are American and there is no
need to tell them how many miles you have
traveled to find your ancestor. Demanding
information and taking counter books to a
reading table is not the accepted manner.

If you enter a repository with a list of
what you want to research and are polite
and abide by the rules, you will be met
more than half way. Your attitude is the
determining factor.

Try to arrange your visit for any month
but August, if your research includes the
National Library and whether for southern
or northern Irish, this is a valuable stop.
In August, the library closes at five every
day and it is closed on Saturday.

In December, the PRO in Belfast is
closed for two weeks.

Major Repositories

Public Record Office, Four Courts, Dublin 7, Ireland located on the river Liffey a few blocks from O'Connell bridge.

Registry of Deeds, Henrietta Street, Dublin 1, Ireland is part of King's Inn and can be entered from Bolton Street through Henrietta Street or from Constitution Hill.

Registrar General's Office, 8 - 11 Lombard Street East, Dublin 2, Ireland is a half block from Pearce Street railroad station and a short walk from the Genealogical Office and National Library.

Genealogical Office, 2 Kildare Street, Dublin 2, Ireland just off Nassau Street and Trinity College.

National Library, Kildare Street, Dublin 2, Ireland is just a few doors from the Genealogical Office and next to the National Museum.

Society of Friends Library, 6 Eustace Street, Dublin 2, Ireland is located between Dame Street and the Quay, a few blocks from Trinity College. Though offically only opened Thursday mornings, if you ring the bell you sometimes can gain access to their library.

Public Record Office of Northern Ireland, 66 Balmoral Avenue, Belfast Northern Ireland BT9 6NY is out of the city center near King's Hall. No bus passes the door and it is a walk to the closest bus stop. Only pencils are allowed in the manuscript room and purses, brief cases, etc. must be stored in a locker before you enter.

Linenhall Library, 17 Donegal Square North, Belfast, Northern Ireland BT1 5GD is downtown right across from city hall. The entrance is a doorway between two shops and not easily recognized.

Presbyterian Historical Society, Church House, Fisherwick Place, Belfast, Northern Ireland, BT1 69W is a short walk from Linenhall Library.

General Register Office, Oxford House, 49 - 55 Chichester Street, Belfast, Northern Ireland BT1 4HF is close to both Linenhall and the Presbyterian Historical Society.

The above list does not include the many numerous local and county libraries which should be visited along with the college libraries.

Suggested Books

This list could consist of hundreds, perhaps even thousands of books, which may not be the best of the bunch and in some cases misleading. As President of Magee Publications, the author could include all the books this company sells but rather the list is limited to those that rate a 10 on the scale from 1-10. Local histories and one name books are not included as this book is for Irish genealogy as a whole rather than putting emphasis on a particular area or surname. Suggestions are included for purchase or using library books. Some listed, should be in every personal library regardless how small.

Passenger and Immigration Lists by P. William Filby lists the name of the passenger, source of arrival record, date and port of arrival, those accompaning the immigrant, ages, etc. In the numerous volumes are over one million entries are indexed for easy searching. This series is found in many libraries and suggest you consult them there.

Famine Immigrant Series: Lists of Irish Immigrants Arriving at the Port of New

York, 1846 - 1851 edited by Ira A. Glazier. This series of books should be used with a double dose of imagination. The original manifests contain many spelling errors coupled with transcribing errors necessitate caution. Try looking for the surname with different vowels and Rs and Bs as capital letters are often in error. If you find your ancestor, write for a copy of the passenger list to the National Archives to assure accuracy. Many libraries have this ongoing series of books.

Irish and Scotch-Irish Ancestral Research by Margaret D. Falley. This two volume work is considered the "Bible" for Irish researchers but not the final word as the books were completed in the early 1960s and many manuscripts, etc. have been added to the collections of Irish repositories. Though readily available at libraries, the serious researcher will soon decide, after frequent trips to the library, that it is better to have the set at home.

Handbook on Irish Genealogy by Heraldic Artists was originally printed in 1970 and updated in 1984. The latest edition with a green cover is indexed and contains the latest addresses of repositories. This is a basic introduction to Irish Research. Though the information given for research on this side of the ocean is incomplete, the maps of each county showing baronies and parishes and the listing of parish registers makes this an important purchase for every Irish researcher.

Irish Genealogist: A Record Finder edited by Donal Begley might be called a sequel to the "Handbook". Chapters are devoted to Wills, Census records and substitutes, Gravestone Inscriptions,

Newspapers, Directories, Miscellaneous Sources, etc. Many manuscripts listed are not found in the Falley books. However, more information is provided on southern rather than northern sources. An excellent book to have on hand when planning research lists for each repository in Ireland but still should be supplemented by the Hayes books and card catalogs.

The <u>Gill History of Ireland Series</u> of eleven volumes by various authors. These books start with Ireland before the Vikings and continue into the twentieth century. An authoritative history written by noted Irish historians published in paperback. Start with the volume that covers the period of your ancestor's migration and work back in time. A must for the serious genealogist!

Should you have any difficulty locating these books, write the author of this book c/o Magee Publications. The address will be found in this book. Please enclose a self addressed stamped envelope.

Book Stores

Many people have inquired where they can obtain copies of out of print books or books on a particular parish or county. In the following list are my favorite book stores. Each year I seem to acquire at least 10 more pounds of books. To avoid carrying this weight around the country, I mail them home. The Post Office (G.P.O.) on O'Connell Street at the corner of Henry Street is open on Saturdays. Some of the shops listed will mail your purchases for you. In fact, several booksellers publish a catalog and mail order constitutes a large percentage of their business.

Fred Hanna Ltd., 27-28-29 Nassau Street, Dublin 2 is located across the street from the side entrance to Trinity College and a few blocks from the National Library. On the ground floor is a large Irish section of new books. The used book section in the basement usually contains many out of print books which are difficult to find but the prices tend to be high. Hanna's has two separate stores. The hard back store closest to Dawson Street is where you will find the above. Though they do not publish a catalog, inquires about a particular book are answered. Hanna's closes at 1:00 PM. on Saturdays

Hodges & Figgis, Dawson Street, Dublin 2 is around the corner from Hanna's, next to Brown Thomas' Department Store. The Irish section is on the first floor (one flight up from the ground floor). Many regional histories, Irish Manuscripts Commission publications and much more. In the basement are books on sale and worth a visit. They also respond to inquiries on a particular book by mail. In recent years, they have extended their opening hours on Saturdays.

Eason & Son is a large bookseller with many stores in Dublin and vicinity. The best selection is at their store on O'Connell Street at the corner of Abbey Street. They do not handle used books. They are open until 5:00 PM on Saturdays.

Roberts Books, St. Kiernan Street, Kilkenny, Co. Kilkenny has many used books and are in the process of reprinting county histories which have been out of print for almost 100 years.

C.P. Hyland Antiquarian Bookseller, The Old Rectory, Wallstown, Castletownroche, Co. Cork, near Mallow, has a large selection of used books. They publish a catalog which everyone should request.

Kenny's Book Store, High Stret, Galway, Co. Galway is a short walk from Eyre Square. The ground floor contains a very large selection of new and used books for genealogists and historians. Ask someone to take you upstairs where they have old maps, prints, etc. On the top floor, they have old copies of periodicals and books that have not been priced. Write and request their catalog.

Emerald Isle Books, 539 Antrim Road, Belfast BT15 3BU is out of City Centre on the main road to Larne. Their selection of used books of interest to genealogists and historians is the best in Northern Ireland. They publish a catalog which you should request.

When trying to obtain a book on an area in Northern Ireland, you may find it more rapidly in the Republic and vice versa. The natives of the area in which a store is located purchase local histories and genealogies. The out of the area books remain on the shelves longer. If, after writing to these booksellers, you still are unable to find the book you need; write the National Library or Linenhall Library. They can photocopy a book if the copyright has expired.

Local History Societies

Many of the organizations listed publish a journal or newsletter and some have produced histories on the local area. Some of the publications are more historical in content rather than genealogical. Many can give you the name of a local researcher. Some counties do not appear on the following list because the writer is not aware of a local society. A society in a neighboring county may be able to provide an address of a local society or researcher. A society whose interest includes other counties is listed under the counties of known interest.

COUNTY ANTRIM

ANTRIM HISTORICAL SOCIETY
Wm. Canning, Dunsilly Lodge, Dunsilly, Co. Antrim, Northern Ireland

BALLYCLARE HISTORICAL SOCIETY
Mrs. L. Weatherup, 689 Doagh Road, Newtownabbey, Co. Antrim, Northern Ireland

CARRICKFERGUS AND DISTRICT HISTORICAL SOCIETY
Mrs. D. Corcoran, 64 Knocksallagh Park,

Greenisland, Co. Antrim, Northern Ireland

EAST BELFAST HISTORICAL SOCIETY
Mr. J. Patton, 309 Old Holywood Road, Holywood, Co. Down, Northern Ireland

GLENS OF ANTRIM HISTORICAL SOCIETY
Mrs. B. McKay, Gruig, Cushendall, Co. Antrim, Northern Ireland

KILLULTAGH HISTORICAL SOCIETY
Mr. T. Lamb, 16 Camlin Park, Crumlin, Co. Antrim, Northern Ireland

LARNE AND DISTRICT HISTORICAL SOCIETY
Mrs. A. Barron, 14 Browndod Road, Millbrook, Larne, Co. Antrim, Northern Ireland

LISBURN HISTORICAL SOCIETY
Miss S. Adams, 27 Sunnyhill Park, Dunmurry, Belfast, Northern Ireland

NORTH BELFAST HISTORICAL SOCIETY
Miss N. Carse, 5 Chichester Court, Belfast, Northern Ireland

WEST BELFAST HISTORICAL SOCIETY
Miss M. C. Smith, 27 Cavendish Street, Belfast, Northern Ireland

COUNTY ARMAGH

ARMAGH DIOCESE HISTORICAL SOCIETY/CUMANN SEANSHAIS ARD MHACHA
Dr. J. B. Walsh, 14 Ashley Park, Armagh, Northern Ireland

CRAIGAVON HISTORICAL SOCIETY
D. B. Cassells, 2 Cherryville Park, Upper Toberhewney, Lurgan, Co. Armagh, Northern Ireland

CREGGAN HISTORICAL SOCIETY
Mrs. G. Hanratty, Teer, Crossmaglen, Co. Armagh, Northern Ireland

COUNTY CARLOW

COUNTY CARLOW HERITAGE SOCIETY
Mr. Liam O'Ceallaigh, 20 Riverside, Carlow, Ireland

OLD CARLOW SOCIETY
Mr Sean O'Leary, Arus na Greine, Montgomery Street, Carlow, Ireland

ST. MULLINS MUINTIR na TIRE HISTORICAL SOCIETY
Mr. Pat Doyle, Newtown Borris, Co. Carlow, Ireland

COUNTY CAVAN

BREIFNE HISTORICAL SOCIETY/CUMANN SEANCHAIS BHREIFNE
Mrs. B. Foy, Swellan Lower, Cavan, Ireland

COUNTY CLARE

CLARE ARCHAEOLOGICAL AND HISTORICAL SOCIETY
Sister Francis O'Dwyner, Colaiste Muire, College Road, Emmis, Co. Clare, Ireland

COROFIN HERITAGE CENTER
Corofin Heritage Center, Corofin, Co. Clare, Ireland

SHANNON ARCHAEOLOGICAL AND HISTORICAL SOCIETY
Mrs. Monica O'Brien, Mount Arley, Drumlin,

Newmarket-on-Fergus, Co. Clare, Ireland

TULLOWPHELIM HISTORIC SOCIETY
Mr. John Keogh, 12 St. Patrick's Park,
Tullow, Co. Clare, Ireland

COUNTY CORK

CUMANN SEANCHAIS na BANNDAN
Mr. Patrick Caniffe, Bawnishal, Hare Hill,
Bandon, Co. Cork, Ireland

CANOVEE HISTORICAL AND ARCHAEOLOGICAL
SOCIETY
Mrs. Sheila Cronin, Caum, Carrigadrohid,
Co. Cork, Ireland

CORK HISTORICAL AND ARCHAEOLOGICAL SOCIETY
Mr. Patrick Holohan, Ballysheehy Lodge,
Clogheen, Co. Cork, Ireland

GREAT ISLAND HISTORICAL SOCIETY
Tim Cadogan, Cork Co. Library, Farranalea
Road, Cork, Ireland

TIMOLEAGUE HISTORICAL SOCIETY
Mr. Robert Travers, Timoleague House,
Bandon, Co. Cork, Ireland

COUNTY DERRY (LONDONDERRY)

BALLINASCREEN HISTORICAL SOCIETY
Miss J. Johnston, Magherafelt Road,
Draperstown, Co. Derry, Northern Ireland

COLERAINE HISTORICAL SOCIETY
F. Agnew, 2 Newlands Crescent, Portstewart,
Co. Derry, Northern Ireland

KILREA HISTORICAL SOCIETY
Mrs. M. Lenox, Drumane, Kilrea, Co. Derry,

Northern Ireland

ROE VALLEY HISTORICAL SOCIETY
Mrs. M. Lueg, Trust Cottage, Limavady, Co.
Derry, Northern Ireland

SOUTH DERRY HISTORICAL SOCIETY
Mrs. N. O'Connor, 7 Highfield Crescent,
Magherafelt, Co. Derry, Northern Ireland

COUNTY DONEGAL

COUNTY DONEGAL HISTORICAL SOCIETY/CUMANN
SEANCHAIS DHUN NA NGALL
Mrs. K. Emerson, 61 Cluain Barron,
Ballyshannon, Co. Donegal, Ireland

COUNTY DOWN

ARDS HISTORICAL SOCIETY
Mr. T. R. Ward, 1 Bowmount Park,
Newtownards, Co. Down, Northern Ireland

BALLYNAHINCH HISTORICAL SOCIETY
D. Wightman, The Croft, 15 Dunmore Road,
The Spa, Ballynahinch, Co. Down, Northern
Ireland

BANBRIDGE AND DISTRICT HISTORICAL SOCIETY
F. Downey, 64 Chinauley Park, Banbridge,
Co. Down, Northern Ireland

BANGOR HISTORICAL SOCIETY
J. McCormick, 282 Seacliff Road, Bangor,
Co. Down, Northern Ireland

THE DOWNE SOCIETY
Miss R. Baillie, 100 Ballynahinch Road,
Crossgar, Co. Down, Northern Ireland

EAST BELFAST HISTORICAL SOCIETY
Mr. J. Patton, 309 Old Holywood Road,
Holywood, Co. Down, Northern Ireland

KILLYLEAGH FAMILY HISTORY SOCIETY
Miss J. O. Bain, 1A Net Walk, Killyleagh,
Co. Down, Northern Ireland

KINGDOM OF MOURNE SOCIETY
Mr. A. Dorna, Springwell House, Mullartown,
Annalog, Co. Down, Northern Ireland

LECALE HISTORICAL SOCIETY
Mr. R. J. Gifford, 5 The Quoile Brae,
Downpatrick, Co. Down, Northern Ireland

OLD NEWRY SOCIETY
Mrs. G. McCoy, Homestead, Jonesboro, Newry,
Co. Down, Northern Ireland

POYNTZPASS AND DISTRICT HISTORICAL SOCIETY
Mrs. B. Heron, 'St. Jude', William Street.
Poyntzpass, Co. Down, Northern Ireland

RATHFRILAND HISTORICAL SOCIETY
Mrs. M. Harbinson, 34 Downpatrick Street,
Rathfriland, Co. Down, Northern Ireland

SAINTFIELD HERITAGE SOCIETY
Miss E. M. Minnis, 16 Moyra Drive,
Saintfield, Co. Down, Northern Ireland

UPPER ARDS HISTORICAL SOCIETY
Mr. R. Oram, Tara, Portaferry, Co. Down,
Northern Ireland

WARRENPOINT HISTORICAL SOCIETY
Miss E. Murray, 20 Pinewood Hill,
Warrenpoint, Co. Down, Northern Ireland

COUNTY DUBLIN

CLONDALKIN HISTORY SOCIETY
Miss Aileen Gourley, 11 Lealand, Bawnogue,
Clondalkin, Co. Dublin, Ireland

DUBLIN ARCHAEOLOGICAL SOCIETY
Ms Jane Behan, 54 Meadowbrook, Baldoyle,
Dublin 13, Ireland

DUN LAOGHAIRE BOROUGH HISTORICAL SOCIETY
Mr. Dermot Dwyer, 35 Glenageary Woods, Dun
Laoghaire, Co. Dublin, Ireland

FOXROCK LOCAL HISTORY CLUB
Mr. Geoffrey Johnson, 74 Clonkeen Drive,
Foxrock, Dublin 18, Ireland

LUCAN HISTORICAL SOCIETY
Mr. Glascorr Symes, c/o The King's
Hospital, Palmerston, Co. Dublin, Ireland

RATHMICHAEL HISTORICAL SOCIETY
Ms Gwendoline Guildford, 4 Springfield
Park, Foxrock, Dublin 18, Ireland

COUNTY GALWAY

OLD GALWAY SOCIETY
Mrs. D. Crombie, Garraun Lower, Maree,
Oranmore, Co. Galway

OFFALY HISTORICAL SOCIETY
Mr. James Scully, St. Rynagh's National
School, Banagher, Co. Offaly, Ireland

KILBEGNET-BALLINAKILLA HISTORICAL SOCIETY
Laurence Kilcommins, Creggs, Co. Galway,
Ireland

COUNTY KERRY

KILLORGLIN HISTORY AND FOLKLORE SOCIETY
Mrs. Jo. Scanlon, Sun Hill, Killorglin, Co.
Kerry, Ireland

COUNTY KILKENNY

KILKENNY ARCHAEOLOGICAL SOCIETY
Mrs. M. Phelan, 10 College Road, Kilkenny,
Ireland

TULLAHERIN PARISH HERITAGE SOCIETY
Mrs. Peggy Walpole, Thomastown Road,
Bennetsbridge, Co. Kilkenny, Ireland

COUNTY LAOIS (QUEEN'S)

LAOIS HERITAGE SOCIETY
Mrs. Matilda Cooney, Monamanry,
Luggacurran, Portlaoise, Co. Laois,
Ireland

OFFALY HISTORICAL SOCIETY
Mr. James Scully, St. Rynagh's National
School, Banagher, Co. Offaly, Ireland

COUNTY LIMERICK

NEWCASTLE WEST HISTORICAL SOCIETY
Mr. John Cussen, Newcastle West, Co.
Limerick, Ireland

THOMOND ARCHAEOLOGICAL SOCIETY
Rev. John Leonard, 9 Castletroy Heights,
Limerick, Ireland

COUNTY LONGFORD

LONGFORD HISTORICAL SOCIETY
Mr. Jude Flynn, Aughadegnan, Longford,
Ireland

COUNTY LOUTH

OLD DROGHEDA SOCIETY
Mrs Moira Corcoran, 5 Brushrod Avenue,
Drogheda, Co. Louth, Ireland

OLD DUNDALK SOCIETY
Miss M. Wilson, 13 St. Mary's Road,
Dundalk, Co. Louth, Ireland

COUNTY LOUTH ARCHAEOLOGICAL AND HISTORICAL
SOCIETY
Mr. Noel Ross, 5 Oliver Plunkett Park,
Dundalk, Co. Louth, Ireland

COUNTY MAYO

WESTPORT HISTORICAL SOCIETY
Mr. Peadar O'Flanagan, Bridge Street,
Westport, Co. Mayo, Ireland

COUNTY MEATH

MEATH ARCHAEOLOGICAL AND HISTORICAL
SOCIETY
Mr. William Battersby, 5 Ludlow Street,
Navan, Co. Meath, Ireland

COUNTY OFFALY (KING'S)

BIRR HISTORICAL SOCIETY
Mrs. Margaret Hogan, Hillside, Birr, Co.

Offaly, Ireland

OFFALY HISTORICAL SOCIETY
Mr. James Scully, St. Rynagh's National
School, Banagher, Co. Offaly, Ireland

TULLAMORE HISTORICAL SOCIETY
Mr. Michael Byrne, Convent View, Tullamore,
Co. Offaly, Ireland

COUNTY ROSCOMMON

COUNTY ROSCOMMON HISTORICAL AND
ARCHAEOLOGICAL SOCIETY
Mr. Michael Kelly, Edenaun, Elphin, Co.
Roscommon, Ireland

COUNTY TIPPERARY

NENAGH DISTRICT HERITAGE SOCIETY
Mrs. Geraldine McNulty, Mount Pleasant,
Ballymackey, Nenagh, Co. Tipperary,
Ireland.

OFFALY HISTORICAL SOCIETY
Mr. James Scully, St. Rynagh's National
School, Banagher, Co. Offaly, Ireland

ORMOND HISTORICAL SOCIETY
Dr. Denise Foulkes, Stoneyhigh,
Gortlandroe, Nenagh, Co. Tipperary,
Ireland

ROSCREA HERITAGE SOCIETY
Mrs. Carmel Cunningham, Parkmore, Rocrea,
Co. Tipperary, Ireland

TEMPLEMORE HISTORICAL SOCIETY
Mr. Donal J. O'Regan, Manna, Templemore,
Co. Tipperary, Ireland

COUNTY TYRONE

CLOGHER HISTORICAL SOCIETY/CUMANN SEANCHAIS CLOCHAIR
J. I. D. Johnston, Corick, Clogher, Co. Tyrone, Northern Ireland

DONAGHMORE HISTORICAL SOCIETY
P. H. Rafferty, St. Patrick's Boys Secondary School, 41 Killymeal Road, Dungannon, Co. Tyrone, Northern Ireland

STEWARTSTOWN HISTORICAL SOCIETY
Mrs. J. F. Laverty, The Castle Farm, Stewartstown, Co. Tyrone, Northern Ireland

WEST TYRONE HISTORICAL SOCIETY
Mr. J. Gilmour, Ulster-American Folk Park, Camphill, Omagh, Co. Tyrone, Northern Ireland

COUNTY WATERFORD

WATERFORD LITERARY AND HISTORICAL SOCIETY
Miss P. Walsh, Cliff Grange, Tramore, Co. Waterford, Ireland

OLD WATERFORD SOCIETY
Mrs. Nellie Croke, 208 Viewmount Park, Waterford, Ireland

COUNTY WESTMEATH

OLD ATHLONE SOCIETY
Miss N. C. Egan, 'Lara' Court, Devenish, Athlone, Co. Westmeath, Ireland

MOATE HISTORICAL SOCIETY
Mr. Jeremiah Sheehan, 'Avila', Moate, Co. Westmeath, Ireland

COUNTY WEXFORD

NEW ROSS LITERARY AND HISTORICAL SOCIETY
Mr. James Doyle, Ard Ross, New Ross, Co. Wexford, Ireland

UI CINSEALAIGH HISTORICAL SOCIETY
Rev. M. Glynn, St. Aiden's, Enniscorthy, Co. Wexford, Ireland

COUNTY WICKLOW

ARKLOW HISTORICAL SOCIETY
Mrs. Mae Greene, 23 St. Peter's Place, Arklow, Co. Wicklow, Ireland

CUALANN HISTORICAL SOCIETY
Mr. Arthur Flynn, 26 Rosslyn, Killarney Road, Bray, Co. Wicklow, Ireland

RATHDANGAN HISTORICAL SOCIETY
Ms Kathleen P. Cullen, Killamoat, Rathdangan, Co. Wicklow, Ireland

WEST WICKLOW HISTORICAL SOCIETY
Mrs Maeve Baker, Ladystown, Rathvilly, Co. Carlow, Ireland

One Last Word

Genealogy is more than just the bare dates, etc. It is knowledge of the country discovered through the reading of histories, both local and national. Historians may not be genealogists but every genealogist should be historian. Study, read and reread everything you can find on the time period when your ancestor migrated. Get a feel for the times and look for clues for possible research. Americans and Canadians are familiar with the histories of their countries and those dates which had to be learned in school provide clues for sending for military records, etc. Yet, it is most convenient not to know about the country from which your ancestor came from. The dates in Irish history such as 1689, 1798, 1847 should be firmly etched in your memory. Learn who the Wild Geese were and where they went. Your pursuit of Irish history will pay off in genealogical success time and time again.

It should be the goal of everyone who is researching an Irish ancestor to visit the Emerald Isle. One can get research done by mail and microfilms, but Irish roots were born in the soil and the turf of that beautiful land across the sea. Those who do have ancestors born in Ireland are truly blessed when their research carries them to Ireland. And the land will always beckon you to go and once you go to the country and meet the Irish, it will make you want to go again and again. Ireland is unique among the European countries because they welcome Americans, Canadians, Australians and New Zealanders as long lost brothers which they probably are.

As hospitable as they are, they are still Irish to whom time has no meaning. Hurrying is what causes all the high blood pressure and heart attacks among Americans and they maintain their own pace. Don't try to fight it! Slow down and enjoy it knowing your ancestor probably went at the same pace.

Ireland is castles, keeps, round towers, monasteries, abbeys, limestone hills and green is found in 40 shades, at least. But the thatch roof cottages are quickly disappearing from the scene being replaced by modern bungalows. Don't wait too long if you have hopes of finding the old ancestral cottage.

There are no troubles in the 26 counties of the Republic of Ireland and though the media reports each and every incident in Northern Ireland, this writer has not seen one bit of trouble in the north. Don't wait for the disagreement to end as it could be a wait. It's been going on for over 300 years, so don't hold your breath. Since less tourists go to Northern Ireland, the hospitality and welcome is usually that much warmer.

Tourists in Ireland are greeted with the Gaelic phrase "Cead Mille Failte" (a hundred thousand welcomes). Through this book, the author extends "Cead Mille Failte" to the world of Irish Genealogy. Happy Hunting!